Forward

God is Within Me is an inspiring and transformative journey into the depths of faith, self-discovery, and divine purpose. This book encourages readers to explore their inner lives, shedding light on the profound truth that each of us is guided, loved, and supported by a presence greater than ourselves. Through powerful reflections, personal anecdotes, and thought-provoking questions, each chapter addresses universal themes that resonate deeply within us all.

From understanding our self-worth to building meaningful friendships, from persevering through challenges to trusting in the divine path laid out before us, *God is Within Me* tackles the real-life issues we all face. These are the moments when we may feel inadequate or lost, but they also hold the potential for growth, joy, and a renewed sense of purpose. As readers move through the chapters, they'll find practical guidance on how to overcome feelings of self-doubt, insights into building a resilient faith, and encouragement to live in harmony with their true calling.

This book is more than just a collection of reflections; it's a spiritual companion for those seeking strength, reassurance, and connection to their faith. Whether you're looking to deepen your relationship with God, nurture a sense of inner peace, or simply find comfort in the knowledge that you are never alone, *God is Within Me* offers a path forward. Through its exploration of topics such as the importance of grace, the beauty of surrender, and the power of hope, the book provides readers with a roadmap to live fully, love deeply, and walk confidently in their divine purpose.

Dive into this journey and discover how you, too, can embrace your unique calling. Learn to trust the journey, build enduring relationships, and face each day with courage and conviction, knowing that God's love and guidance are with you every step of the way. With *God is Within Me*, you'll find a sanctuary of faith and a testament to the strength that resides within each of us, a reminder that we are all connected, supported, and cherished by a divine presence.

TABLE OF CONTENTS

We're All In This Together	3
Am I Enough?	4-5
Faith is Your Rope– Hang on Help is on the Way!	6
Alone But Not Lonely	7
Friends, How Many of us Have Them?	8
Overcomer	9
Called to Give it to the Youth	10-11
Dear God—Am I Good Enough?	12
Walking in God's Purpose!	13
Friendships can come in Seasons and that's Okay!	14-15
Friends, How Many of Us Have Them?	16-17
God's Team	18
How Do You Measure Your Success?	19
Travelers in the Fog	20-21
The Song of Gratitude	22
Give Way To Your Destiny!	23
Putting Faith in God Will Always Make Things Happen	24-25
Those People!	26-27
The Timing of Transformation	28-29
Keep Your Vision	30-31
A Healthy MIND, BODY, and SOUL	32-33
Christlike in Social Media	34-35
Let Him Guide You!	36-37
He Has The Blueprint!	38-39
Wisdom-God's Guarantee!	40-41
It's Okay To Mourn	41
Better Than The Beginning	42-43

We're All In This Together

Suppose one of you wants to build a tower. Won't you first sit down and estimate the cost to see if you have enough money to complete it?" (NIV Luke 14:28).

I was raised to always be a willing servant. I was also raised to go above and beyond in everything I do. I love the values I was raised with. However, I sometimes forget that I need to take care of myself first. Not in a self-centered way but God's way. I need to make time to spend with my creator, giving Him first place I my life. Before I go out to save the world, I have to save myself by going above and beyond for myself. This method helps me to feel like I'm not alone and we're all in this together. I'm no expert keyboard player, but I'd like to think of us as interdependent like the keys on a piano. No single key is more important than the other. When played together in harmony, something beautiful is produced.

The scripture Luke 14:28, discusses the need to plan finances for material things. This application can be used to prioritize how we are to deal with caring for ourselves before burning out taking care of others. Being selfless is admirable. Yet, I can't do give all of myself away if I have nothing to give. I must ask if I've given God the first fruits of my life. I also have to ask if I've given myself enough love, care, nourishment, rest, and prayer.

Lately, I haven't done so, and the result has left me feeling incomplete. That incomplete feeling led me down one of the deepest self-loathing spirals I have ever been in.

For almost two weeks, I questioned whether staying alive was beneficial anymore. I'm still working my way out of that spiral. I'm learning to fund my personal value. This way I can effectively manage my mind, body, and soul in a way that allows me to honor my upbringing without compromising myself in the process.

Prayer: Dear Lord, please hear me when I call on you. I sometimes struggle with caring for myself. Will you help me? Bless our time together so I can be strengthened. Help me to fill up my tank by being with you and recharging my batteries. This way I can better pour into others. Thank you. Amen.

Am I Enough?

But he said to me, "My grace is sufficient for you, for my power is made perfect in weakness." Therefore, I will boast all the more gladly about my weaknesses, so that Christ's power may rest on me. That is why, for Christ's sake, I delight in weaknesses, in insults, in hardships, in persecutions, in difficulties. For when I am weak, then I am strong (2nd Corinthians 12:9-10 NIV

Growing up, I was always fond of superheroes. It was not the special powers or weapons that appealed to me. I thought all those things were cool, but I mostly fell in love with the idea that someone would dedicate their whole life to helping others who could not help themselves.

You see in that time, my parents' two biggest lessons for me were to have a servant's heart and to always go above and beyond in a task. I thank my parents dearly for instilling those values in me because it created the person that I am today. I found my way to teaching, during a global pandemic no-less, because of them. The problem lies in the fact that I connected those values to how I could be a real-life superhero.

I expect more of myself than anyone. I am also my own worst critic. I can make others happy with my work, but I still question how much more I could have done to be better. I have many days where I question if I am good enough to handle this field I've chosen. In most aspects of my life I question whether or not I am enough. Everything came to a head a couple of weeks ago when I burst into tears after a meeting over that one question. My Assistant Principal called me into her office after the school day was over to discuss my feelings. The one thing that has stuck with me from that meeting is her telling me that I don't have to be Superwoman all the time. It's ok to just be Clark Kent. It smacked me like a ton of bricks. I had been trying so hard and for so long to be the best I can at everything that I forgot that my favorite heroes never stayed in their hero form 24/7. Most of them went about their daily lives in their normal form until the occasion called for them to be a hero.

Cont.. Am I Enough?

The scripture again…*2 Corinthians 12:9-10 says, "But he said to me, 'My grace is sufficient for you, for my power is made perfect in weakness'. Therefore, I will boast all the more gladly about my weaknesses, so that Christ's power may rest on me. That is why, for Christ's sake, I delight in weaknesses, in insults, in hardships, in persecutions, in difficulties. For when I am weak, then I am strong."*

One thing I struggle with is giving myself grace. I forget that God grants me at least that much. He understands that I am not a perfect being and that I will have difficulties. I still struggle with my superwoman complex, but I am learning that I don't have to be perfect. By being imperfect, I can let God shine his best.

Prayer: *Father God, I thank you that your grace is sufficient for me. I thank you for the guidance you have given me through your word, my parents, and my vice principal. I ask that you continue to touch other people's lives as you have done mine.*

Faith is Your Rope– Hang on Help is on the Way!

In this you greatly rejoice, though now for a little while, if need be, you have been grieved by various trials, that the genuineness of your faith, being much more precious than gold that perishes, though it is tested by fire, may be found to praise, honor, and glory at the revelation of Jesus Christ, 1 Peter 1:6-7 (NKJV)

Faith is to the mind as love is to the heart. We know that when someone you love hurts you or leaves you, you become broken hearted. That is the same thing that happens to your faith, when things don't go the way you want it to go, it affects your faith in God. I am here to tell you that faith eases a mind overwhelmed by the (hows) and the (whys) of a situation.

Faith brings peace to the chaotic thoughts, worries, and anxieties in your life. Faith is a soothing comfort to the racing mind filled with fear. Faith is a comforting blanket to the mind gone cold with doubt and negativity. Faith empowers a weak mind that does not believe it can overcome a challenge and reassures a gentle mind that is afraid to step out of its comfort zone.

When thought and action alone are not enough to face an obstacle or overcome a challenge, call upon the warrior known as faith. Ephesians 6:16 tells us, "Take up the shield of faith, with which you can extinguish all the flaming arrows of the evil one." For only faith can go where the rational mind cannot and see what the reasoning mind fails to see. This quote comes to mind when I think about my faith and my God, "All who call on God in true faith, earnestly from the heart, will certainly be heard, and will receive what they have asked and desired. – Martin Luther

Prayer: *Heavenly Father, give us hope, give us patience to cope and a reason to keep holding on. Take our trembling hand and give us the power to not let go. Lord give us the faith that will allow us to climb that rope and pull our sister up as well. In your precious son- Jesus' name. Amen!*

Alone But Not Lonely

*HAVE I NOT COMMANDED YOU? BE STRONG AND OF GOOD COURAGE; DO NOT BE AFRAID, NOR BE DISMAYED, FOR THE LORD YOUR GOD IS WITH YOU WHEREVER YOU GO (**JOSHUA 1:9 NKJV**).*

She was so much better at being alone; being alone came more naturally to her. She led a life of deliberate solitude, and if occasional loneliness crept in, she knew how to work her way out… Or even better, how to sink in and absorb its particular comforts. – Cynthia D'Aprix Sweeney

This quote spoke volumes to me as I remembered my 8th grade through 12th grade school years. I was bullied a lot and at one point I just did not want to live. I remember one Saturday morning my parents were out of the house, and I just felt really bad about what I was going through. I remember asking God, "Why can't I have some really good friends that treat me right?" I called my mom, and my parents immediately came home. They talked with me, and then prayed for me. After that, I began to be content with being alone.

Most people think that just because I am now 21, I should have friends and be out on the weekends having a 'life'. At one time I did want to be that person. I was never an outgoing person and I even thought there was a problem with me as to why I was not hanging out with my peers. One night, I felt God in my Spirit and he told me too just be myself. Psalm 4:3 tells me, "But know that the LORD hath set apart him that is godly for himself: the LORD will hear when I call unto him." Knowing this truth gives me comfort and allows me to be content with being alone.

Although I am physically alone without my peers, I am never alone because God is always there. Now I am not saying I dislike people or do not want to hang out with friends. I am just cautious, and I trust God to bring the right Godly friends into my life. Just because someone sees me alone does not mean I am lonely. I always have God there. He is my best friend. Dear family, future friends, future husband…I am content with being alone, but that does not mean I will not be there for you when you need me.

__Prayer:__ Father God, I thank you for being my comforter, counselor, healer, and my friend. I ask that you continue to be all that and so much more in my life. I lift up others who are hurting because they think that they are alone. I pray others feel the same kind of love that you have shown me. Amen

Friends, How Many of us Have Them?

Now when Job's three friends heard of all this evil that had come upon him, they came each from his own place, Eliphaz the Temanite, Bildad the Shuhite, and Zophar the Naamathite. They made an appointment together to come to show him sympathy and comfort him (Job 2:11 ESV).

True friends are usually hard to come by. At least, that has usually been the case for me. I grew up having a different "best friend" every couple of months. I have also never felt badly about it because I can easily make a new friend. Despite that fact, I have been blessed to have found several sets of true friends in my life. When I was in college, I had my first suicide attempt. I had planned on running a red light in front of a semi the next chance I got because it would at least seem like an accident. I never got a chance to be the first person at a red light my entire trip back to campus. I told a few friends when I got back to campus of what I had tried to do. I was not left alone for the rest of the night. I was dragged to go eat out and made to laugh until my belly hurt. One even stayed the night with me to be sure I was okay. They made sure I knew that I was not alone.

I met two very dear friends while living in Dallas a year. After I left, I didn't feel as close to them as we once were. I should have never doubted. The day my father passed, I made one phone call to them and they were at my side within a couple of days. I had friends in town that didn't make an effort to look in after me but here were these ladies that I had not spoken to in a couple months. They came and did as much as they could to comfort, entertain, and distract me. I am forever grateful for their willingness to drop everything and be there.

I truly believe God puts people in our lives so that we are never alone in our suffering. Even to this day with my ever-changing seasons and relationships with people, I constantly find myself having a new person placed in my life to provide counsel and comfort. This year has also been tough for me teaching through a pandemic and teaching multiple grade levels. However, in each placement I have found a new friend to help me emotionally, spiritually, and especially in the classroom.

Prayer: *Lord, help me to always have you as one of my best friends. Give me the wisdom, discernment, and guidance I need to navigate relationships. Show me how to be a good friend. And please show me who my true friends are. Amen*

Overcomer

Psalms 119:11 *Thy word have I hid in mine heart, that I might not sin against thee.*

This has been my favorite scripture since I was in the 4th grade. As I think back on my early childhood to now, I have no regrets of following the word of the Lord. I can still remember going home after school and reading this scripture every day. I remember some kids being unkind to me. But I remembered my teachings from my parents as it relates to the love of God and his word. And this always brought me through. I overcame.

Being diagnosed with dyslexia and learning how to deal with it had challenges. With the help of my parents and God, I was able to overcome it. You see, words are a powerful thing when it comes to faith. I had my parents always speaking blessings over me. I also had the word of God inside me. I could call upon the Lord to get me through any situation I was in.

With my strong faith in God, I realize I never have to be a perfect person who goes to church every time the doors are open. Neither do I have to be a perfect person who knows how to pray an elaborate prayer. The same truth is available to all of us. All we need are our *words* and we can speak to God anytime we need him and call on His words from the bible. We can then get through the trials of this life, with God on our side.

Prayer: *Dear God I come to you as humble as I can thanking you for your help in navigating my way through life. I ask that you keep your hand of protection on every young person in my life. I ask that you send help, hope and healing their way to lead and guide them to your way of living. In Jesus' name I pray. Amen*

Called to Give it to the Youth

2nd Timothy 3:14 – 17 NIV says, "14 But as for you, continue in what you have learned and have become convinced of, because you know those from whom you learned it, 15 and how from infancy you have known the Holy Scriptures, which are able to make you wise for salvation through faith in Christ Jesus. 16 All Scripture is God-breathed and is useful for teaching, rebuking, correcting and training in righteousness, 17 so that the servant of God may be thoroughly equipped for every good work."

In 2018, I was at a women's retreat in Texas with my mother and a few other women from our church. The morning of our second day I found myself silently complaining about not being prophesied to like others the night before. I wanted to know where I was supposed to go in life but, I didn't want to ask. It felt like it wouldn't be a genuine calling if I had to. Later, that afternoon I got what I wanted. I was told simply to, "give it to the youth." I knew in my spirit those words meant the field of education.

Fast forward to 2020 where I was hired at a school where I'd previously been a substitute teacher. I'd never taken an education class but there I was because it is what I was called to do. Though, I knew I would have challenges. Yet, I also knew the word of God said I was equipped for every good work (2nd Tim 3).

I asked myself the question many times: What does it look like when God strengthens me? I would soon find out it was a process. First, I had to take the steps to get hired. Then, I had to learn to teach online. Finally, I realized it means we do our part in equipping ourselves, but He gives you the tools needed to get the job done.

Cont...Called to Give it to the Youth

As we go through this period of a "new normal," I've noticed how tough it is on my students. We are no longer in the classroom each day. Some children don't have the most conducive environments to learn in. A few are dealing with the real impacts of this virus. They now realize this isn't about staying home and playing on the computer, it's about getting an education in a different way.

The question I've struggled with lately is: How do I keep my students engaged, motivated, and uplifted? I can't give them the hugs and treats that they used to receive freely. I can't share the scriptures that give me daily encouragement. But I can give them what God gave me. I can give them the tools they need to get through the rest of the school year. I can teach them and remind them of the skills and strategies that we've already reviewed. I can be there for them as a guide or a listening ear. I can help them access the tools they need to accomplish tasks on their own. I can be a "servant of God thoroughly equipped for every good work."

Prayer: *Father God, I thank you for your love and guidance. I thank you for your signs and wonders that you have given your people in this world. I ask that you continue to lead and guide your people to build upon the gifts you give them to help others along the way. In your son Jesus' name, I pray. Amen.*

Dear God—Am I Good Enough?

Your beauty should not come from outward adornment, such as elaborate hairstyles and the wearing of gold jewelry or fine clothes. Rather, it should be that of your inner self, the unfading beauty of a gentle and quiet spirit, which is of great worth in God's sight (1st Peter 3:3-4 NIV).

I'm sure most of us have heard the saying, "they're pretty on the outside, but they're ugly on the inside." I have struggled with "not feeling good enough," I did not feel pretty on the outside and definitely was not thinking about my inside. Let me explain...since the age of thirteen my medical journey started. I was getting cysts on my breast, underarms, legs, and buttocks. My hair started falling out and just would not grow. Then the weight gain started, and I did not know why. I did not eat a lot and I was active, a cheerleader at that.

It took a while for the doctors to put a name on my medical condition and believe me, I went through several doctors. I later discovered I had Polycystic ovary syndrome (PCOS) and Hidradenitis Suppurativa (HS). I also found out both diseases are incurable. There's nothing I can do about it. Nothing.

I know, 3rd John 1:2 (NKJV) says, *Beloved, I pray that you may prosper in all things and be in health, just as your soul prospers.* Yet, I often think, *am I good enough? Why can't I be healthy?* Because of the surgeries I have had, and the weight gain I've been struggling with, I've developed lots of insecurities regarding my body. I find myself wondering if I'll ever get married and if a man would accept me the way I am.

As a young person who has hopes of being married someday, being accepted the way you are is important and brings paralyzing doubts to my mind. Then the Lord put these words in my spirit: "Your mind is healthy. It's not your shape, hair, or other things that make you beautiful. It's your love for me and the way you show my love toward others." I'm not saying I don't still struggle, but God's affirming words in the Bible and in my spirit make all the difference in letting me know, *I am good enough.*

Prayer: *Father God, thank you for being there in my lowest and darkest hours. Thank you for being sunshine in my life. Help me NOT to believe it's my body, hair, glamour, and material things that make me beautiful. Let my beauty within flow from within to be a blessing to others. In Jesus name, Amen!*

Walking in God's Purpose!

"The Lord foils the plans of the nations; he thwarts the purposes of the peoples. But the plans of the Lord stand firm forever, the purposes of his heart through all generations" Psalm 33:10-11 (NIV).

Have you ever had to get to a specific place, pull up the GPS on your phone, look at the directions and say to yourself; I know a better way to get there, so I am going to take that road? But later, after taking your way to the destination, come to find out, there were some roadblocks, and you should have gone the way the GPS told you. However, since you made that choice, you must see your way through the roadblocks to get where you need to be.

This seemed to be the story of my life. Everything I was for or thought I wanted wasn't working out. It felt like every road to get where I wanted to be was blocked for one ridiculous reason after another.

As Christians, we're told to persevere and that those roadblocks are just trials and tribulations we must get through before we get to where we need to be.

Psalm 33:10-11 tells us that God deliberately blocks all our plans if they do not align with His purpose for us. Isaiah 30:1 tells us that God will obstruct plans made when consulting man instead of him.

Lately, it seems like I'm heading down a smooth path, but this wasn't the case for me a year ago. This wasn't the case even a few months ago. Learning to trust the directions that God has put before me and not trying to go off my inclination has put me in a peaceful place. I am now walking in my purpose.

Prayer: *Father in Heaven, I thank you for a teachable heart. I thank you for the path you have chosen for me. Please continue to be my guide through these travels of my life. In Jesus' name, AMEN!*

Friendships can come in Seasons and that's Okay!

"To everything there is a season, and a time to every purpose under the heaven:"(Ecclesiastes 3:1 KJV).

Friends are not needed to define who you are and the more friends you have will not make you a better person in people's eyes. *Oh, what a friend I have in Jesus!* He will never leave you and will be there through every season of your life.

Just like the bible says, "to everything there is a season." I have experienced my "seasons" with different friends or associates. God allows certain people to come into our lives as a blessing to us, or for us to be a blessing to others. Since the word tells us to: *bless them that curse you, do good to them that hate you, and pray for them which despitefully use you, and persecute you Matthew 5:44 KJV).*

Growing up I had friends that I went through elementary, middle, and high school with. However, after high school we parted ways. It's not that we angrily parted ways. Life took us in separate directions. Our season had run its course.

I have always been laid back. I'm not wired as an outgoing person. Therefore, I've never developed deep friendships easily. Also, I treasure my alone time. Because of this trait, I believe some people misunderstand me, and mistake me as unfriendly.

A good friend is not always a person you grew up with; a good friend is loyal to you, accepts you for who you are during your best of times and during your worst time. A good friend keeps your secrets and they refrain from spreading rumors of their opinion about you. If you are blessed with those types of friendships, cherish them.

Cont...Friendships can come in Seasons and that's Okay!

If you are feeling like you are without any friends and the world hates you, then remember the word in, *John 15:18: If the world hates you, ye know that it hated me before it hated you (KJV)*.

Prayer: *Heavenly Father, I come to You, thankful for all the different friends I have had in my different seasons. I even thank you for the "frenemies" in sheep's clothing. I ask that you help me be a friend like Jesus is to those who need friendship. Thank you for the continual love You show to the friendless. I pray this in Jesus' name, your precious Son. Amen!*

Friends, How Many of Us Have Them?

Now when Job's three friends heard of all this evil that had come upon him, they came each from his own place, Eliphaz the Temanite, Bildad the Shuhite, and Zophar the Naamathite. They made an appointment together to come to show him sympathy and comfort him (Job 2:11 ESV).

True friends are usually hard to come by. At least, that has usually been the case for me. I grew up having a different "best friend" every couple of months. I have also never felt badly about it because I can easily make a new friend. Despite that fact, I have been blessed to have found several sets of true friends in my life. When I was in college, I had my first suicide attempt. I had planned on running a red light in front of a semi the next chance I got because it would at least seem like an accident. I never got a chance to be the first person at a red light my entire trip back to campus. I told a few friends when I got back to campus of what I had tried to do. I was not left alone for the rest of the night. I was dragged to go eat out and made to laugh until my belly hurt. One even stayed the night with me to be sure I was okay. They made sure I knew that I was not alone.

I met two very dear friends while living in Dallas a year. After I left, I didn't feel as close to them as we once were. I should have never doubted. The day my father passed, I made one phone call to them and they were at my side within a couple of days. I had friends in town that didn't make an effort to look in after me but here were these ladies that I had not spoken to in a couple months. They came and did as much as they could to comfort, entertain, and distract me. I am forever grateful for their willingness to drop everything and be there.

Friends, How Many of Us Have Them?

I truly believe God puts people in our lives so that we are never alone in our suffering. Even to this day with my ever-changing seasons and relationships with people, I constantly find myself having a new person placed in my life to provide counsel and comfort. This year has also been tough for me teaching through a pandemic and teaching multiple grade levels. However, in each placement I have found a new friend to help me emotionally, spiritually, and especially in the classroom.

Prayer: *Lord, help me to always have you as one of my best friends. Give me the wisdom, discernment, and guidance I need to navigate relationships. Show me how to be a good friend. And please show me who my true friends are. Amen*

God's Team

For by the grace given me I say to every one of you: Do not think of yourself more highly than you ought, but rather think of yourself with sober judgment, in accordance with the faith God has distributed to each of you (Romans 12:3 NIV).

"Guarding, that's what it comes down to," said Booker a member of the 2021 men's Olympic basketball team for the USA during an interview after the game that earned his team a spot to compete for gold. Although the USA team had fallen behind by as many as 15 points in the second quarter and trailed behind by three points by halftime, team USA made a remarkable comeback! They progressed to compete for a gold medal by winning the game against Australia 97-78. After interviewing additional USA players, they agreed with Booker, the offense improved but—the team's defense had made all the difference.

When we look at examples like that of the Team USA athletes playing basketball, it takes everyone working together to get the best outcome possible for the team. Even if one is actually better than the other, it takes all players doing their part in their positions to be successful.

In taking a closer look at basketball, there are five positions to be played during the game. However, despite someone being a good shooter doesn't mean they should negate the other players and always take *that* shot. In fact, other team players might be at a better vantage point to make the shot. Additionally, when the team wins, and certain players score the most points, they don't get the the right to say they won the game for the team, dismissing what the other players did defensively.

This same analogy applies to the saints (no, not my beloved Louisiana team, but team members) of God. We might be one body "in Christ" but there are numerous members. It takes many to serve on God's team. He gives everyone various roles, gifts, and talents. It is up to every member to operate in their role, to love, and lift each other up. In the end, we're all on the same level, made mighty by God to worship Him, bring others to Christ—guarding, each other, that's what it comes down to.

Prayer: *Father God, please help me to play well with others and to have a selfless, forgiving, and grudge-free heart when I'm wronged and hurt. Help me to show Christ and not the disappointments of this life when there are losses and the fiery darts of attack. Help me to love like Jesus and to rejoice with all my heart when I'm victorious! In Jesus name, Amen!*

How Do You Measure Your Success?

'Not by might nor by power, but by my Spirit,' says the Lord Almighty (Zechariah 4:6 NIV).

Many of us believe that to succeed we must be tough, strong, unbending, and even harsh. But God lets us know the secret of our success is because of His spirit. As we live for God, we need to be determined NOT to trust in our OWN strength or abilities. God is the one working behind the scenes to help us achieve success in our jobs, families, relationships, finances, and other areas important to us. We do what we can do and God does the impossible. When we totally depend on God, He works in the power of His Spirit. God is the only one who is all powerful.

When I take a look down memory lane, I recall a time when I was employed at this particular office where evaluations were important Annually, I had to do a self-evaluation, then I would receive one from management. The outcome of the evaluation determined my raise and the success I could achieve in my position.

I thought it was pointless to complete a self-evaluation. I kept thinking, "of course, we'll all give ourselves the highest score possible." But as I began to get honest with myself, I realized there were plenty of things I could improve on.

Just as we would read and do what was required of us from an employee handbook, the same thing is required of us by God. Think about the success God can give us by reading and following the directions in his "employee handbook"—the Bible. He's the all-powerful one who gives us the success we need!

Prayer: *Father God, I thank you for being a present help in every aspect of my life. I thank you for the times you nudge me to evaluate my heart, motives, and most of all your will and word. Amen!*

Travelers in the Fog

"And we know that in all things God works for the good of those who love him, who have been called according to his purpose (Romans 8:28 NIV).

According to the Bureau of Standards in Washington, a dense fog covering seven city blocks to a depth of 100 feet is composed of less than one glass of water. That amount of water is divided into about 60 billion tiny droplets. Yet when those minute particles settle over a city or the countryside, they can almost blot out everything from your sight.

I remember one day I drove out of my driveway headed to work. It was early morning, but it looked as if it was nighttime. I immediately noticed that not only was it dark, but the day was enshrouded in a thick fog. For those of us who've driven in fog before, we just slow down and use more caution, which is what I did.

But this morning, the fog seemed impenetrable. I was tempted to return home or stop after traveling a mile down the road. I then remembered to turn on my fog lights, and the words of my husband echoed in my mind encouraging me to "find the good in each situation." Then God began to speak to my heart and reveal things to me about my walk with him. I learned:

· The fog limits my vision, but there's still a clear path God has for me to travel

· Clarity is achieved when we shine God's light into each situation

· Sometimes the obscured details aren't necessary if God is our guide

· We can recognize the move of the Spirit of God, even when we can't see God or His work clearly

· We can recognize God's handiwork by the shape of His love and mercy.

Cont...Travelers in the Fog

The fog of life can sometimes obscure our view as we travel the road of life and caution must be observed. We may be tempted to return to our old ways or stop on our journey because of discouragement and fear. Most of the time in life, we can only see a few feet ahead. However, we can travel by faith, knowing that the way is sure when we trust God to lead us.

Prayer: Heavenly Father, I thank you for always being the light in the darkness of our travels through this world we are in. I ask that you continue to be our pilot and keep us safe from all hurt, harm, and dangers that are out there. In Jesus Christ's name, I pray. Amen!

The Song of Gratitude

My lips will call out for joy when I sing praises to You. You have set my soul free (Psalm 71:23 NLV).

We didn't talk much during the first couple of hours of the drive. Lost in our thoughts, the miles speed by faster than the past few years after losing dad had. I stared out the window, watching the trees, sky, and cars whiz by, observing the changing landscape. A chill was in the crisp air. I wondered if things would finally feel like home again once we settled into our new state. I felt too exhausted to dream again and too disappointed in people and their empty promises, dread set in. *What if this is another dead end for us?*

While moving to Texas from Florida during our car ride, my mother and I finally turned on the gospel station after hours of silence. Music filled the emptiness in our vehicle and hearts. Soon a peaceful spirit enveloped the car. I took a deep breath, realizing how much I'd missed gospel music and how much it uplifted my spirits. Music has always had a way of penetrating the depth of my soul. I began to feel a deep sense of thankfulness, and the darkness I felt was pierced by the light of gratitude.

As we approached my sister's apartment, I sensed a deep appreciation for the peace experienced despite our unplanned journey and my fight with illness, death, and disappointment.

It occurred to me that Gratitude is a gift God gives us. Expressing thankfulness shows me how to never take anything for granted. I am thankful for what I have and what I receive. Being grateful is a powerful way of drawing close to God.

The bottom line is this:
· Gratitude glorifies God.
· Gratitude puts me in God's will.
· Gratitude brings peace.
· Gratitude draws us to God.

Prayer: *Dear Lord, my lips will call out for joy when I sing praises to You. You have set my soul free. I ask you to show me how to praise you through the storms and keep my heart grateful. Amen!*

Give Way To Your Destiny!

A gift opens the way and ushers the giver into the presence of the great.
Proverbs 18:16 (NIV)

I was taught that you do not go empty-handed to a friend's home. At least not the first time, anyway. It does not have to be anything big or expensive, just something from the heart that can show them you care and that you are thankful for them welcoming you.

God did the same thing before sending us to earth. He bestowed us with a gift to use. As a kid, one of my favorite songs to sing in the church was "I'm Available to You" by Milton Brunson and The Thompson Community Singers. The song speaks of God's gifts and how we can use them to edify and bless others.

When we use the gifts God has given, they open doors and pathways to better things. The problem lies in *not* recognizing our gifts. Sometimes the gifts we're given seem impractical. So, we turn away from them for pursuits deemed more worthy of our time.

Another issue I have struggled with is that the road to my destiny makes me doubt my gift. When it seems like I keep failing and can't move forward, I will give up. This happened again to me recently. However, my mother encouraged me to continue. Even if I didn't get everything perfect the way I wanted, I would at least be able to say it was completed, and that would be enough. I am glad she pushed me to keep moving forward with my destiny.

I exceeded my goal and now have new doors opened, and even ones I thought I had closed myself off from were reopened. This season in my life had me asking myself: "where would you be if you'd continued using your other gifts rather than casting them aside as soon as the road got difficult?" My goal now is to stop blocking myself from the destiny God has for me and utilize the gifts he has given me to do his will.

Prayer: *Father God, I thank you for the gifts you've given me. Please help me to recognize, use, and never discard the gifts you have provided. May I do everything to give you the honor and glory that is due to you. Amen!*

Putting Faith in God Will Always Make Things Happen

"And we know that in all things God works for the good of those who love him, who have been called according to his purpose" (Romans 8:28 NIV).

Recently, I had a conversation with a friend about having faith. We discussed several ways to apply our faith, including finding the right people to be in close fellowship with and finding our purpose. When questioned about how I could be so sure that God would help me find close connections and my purpose, my response was, "I have faith." According to the Oxford dictionary, one of the definitions of faith is complete trust or confidence in someone or something.

In *Mark 11:23 (NIV)*, Jesus tells the disciples, *"Truly I tell you, if anyone says to this mountain, 'Go, throw yourself into the sea,' and does not doubt in their heart, but believes that what they say will happen, it will be done for them."* In context, Jesus had been hungry and cursed a fig tree for not having any fruit. In other words, the tree had the potential to produce fruit, and Jesus had faith that the tree could produce fruit. Yet, the tree didn't produce what it'd been designed to grow by the creator.

The lesson I learned from Mark 11:23 was that it is not enough to say we believe something will happen, but we must trust God that He will make it so. In the conversation with my friend regarding faith, I gave an example of faith by describing how God called me to work with youth. It was the first time I had declared it and believed it. After I said it aloud, things started to happen for me to push me back in the direction of my purpose. I was called in for an interview for a teaching position at a childcare facility. Subsequently, I was offered the job the next day. As I began my training, I was offered a lead teacher position instead. I'm learning it's not enough to ask God for things; I must also trust that the seeds of faith he planted in me will grow as I do my part to flourish.

Cont...Putting Faith in God Will Always Make Things Happen

Going back to the conversation with my friend, I know I can't make anyone believe in God. But what I can do is plant the seeds of faith. It's up to the individual to grow in Christ or not. The scripture in 1 Corinthians 3:5-9 gives us a good illustration of this point: What, after all, is Apollos? And what is Paul? Only servants, through whom you came to believe—as the Lord has assigned to each his task. 6 I planted the seed, Apollos watered it, but God has been making it grow. 7 So neither the one who plants nor the one who waters is anything, but only God, who makes things grow. 8 The one who plants and the one who waters have one purpose, and they will each be rewarded according to their labor. 9 For we are co-workers in God's service; you are God's field, God's building (NIV).

The bottom line is that it's not our job to convince friends to believe in God. We're supposed to plant the seeds, use our faith, and let God do the growth in others.

Prayer: Dear God, thank you for your presence in my life. Thank you for putting me in a position to realize the amount of faith I have in You. I ask that you bless all those struggling with challenges and a lack of faith in their lives. Show me how to nurture relationships with others so I can have an opportunity to sow seeds of faith, and you can reap the harvest of believers. In your son Jesus' name, I pray. Amen!

Those People!

Jesus replied, "Truly I tell you, if you have faith and do not doubt, not only can you do what was done to the fig tree, but also you can say to this mountain, 'Go, throw yourself into the sea,' and it will be done. If you believe, you will receive whatever you ask for in prayer" (Matt 21:21 NIV).

After my husband passed away and the life I once knew crumbled around me, I was forced to confront the reality of certain people in my life. In this journey, I want to address the challenge of dealing with difficult, even unreasonable individuals. I encountered those who spoke hurtful words, those who betrayed my trust by sharing my confidences with others, and those I had supported in their times of need who never once reached out to me in mine. I firmly believe that with God, all things are possible, and that when we ask in prayer, He provides. However, not all things are possible with those who do not carry the love of Jesus within them.

I realized after several poorly attended pity parties, binge eating, binge-watching, and binge crying (that's a real thing. I promise it is) I'd had enough. Certain people weren't going to act in the way I believed they should. It did me no good to confront them over their behavior, lack of support, and judgment.

Concluding that it wasn't my duty to fix people in my life gave me great relief. Through the grace of time and prayer, God revealed to me that my role is to be obedient to Him in how I behave and act to "those" people.

Do you know what I did? I backed away. In some cases, I severed unhealthy relationships to protect what bit of sanity I had left.

To be clear, I'm not suggesting we run out and get a divorce or cut off every family member who upsets us. Most of those issues (unless we're talking physical abuse) can be resolved with a Christian counselor, prayer, and lots of chocolate.

What I'm suggesting is this: amputate toxic relationships from our lives. There I said it. Cut it off. Do it graciously and lovingly but do it, nonetheless.

We must first pursue peace with God and guard everything that seeks to interfere. Therefore, if there're relationships in our lives where "those" people refuse to pursue peace with us, then we may be better off loving them from afar. Even if it's for a time—sometimes apart is better.

We have examples of this in the Bible. For instance, it was clear that Paul and Barnabas had their issues. Acts 15 tells us these men had a "sharp disagreement." That's an excellent way of saying they weren't good together. Those brothers were about to start rumbling, so they took a break from each other.

Cont...Those People!

I'm happy that they eventually worked through their relationship because later in the Bible, we find that they were working together again.

The truth is, as Paul and Barnabas, we must pursue being the person God wants us to be regardless of how others react. That doesn't always mean something as drastic as an amputation. It may mean taking a break from "those" people as we grow in maturity and our relationship with Christ.

Here are a few scriptures and tips I've learned along the way to assist us with the process of dealing with "those" people:

Trust God's Word *"Teach me, O Lord, the way of Your statutes, And I shall observe it to the end.* Pray and ask God, "what am I doing wrong" and to "teach me to communicate, so there are fewer chances of being misunderstood" *(Psalm 27:11 NIV).*

Follow God's Ways *"When my spirit grows faint within me, it is you who watch over my way. In the path where I walk people have hidden a snare for me.* Even when we feel as if the world hates us and we're alone, we must encourage ourselves with the reminder that God is always with us" *(Psalm 142:3 NIV).*

Depend on God's Faithfulness *"The Lord is faithful, who will establish you and guard you against the evil one."* We must trust in God's faithfulness to us by focusing on what is correct and acceptable in his eyes" *(2 Thessalonians 3:3 NIV).*

Every aspect of this walk with God isn't going to feel good. It can be a downright struggle. Nothing about the premature death of my beloved spouse felt good. Neither did the abandonment nor abuse I suffered at the hands of others. Yet, I'm reminded that we must stand on *Isaiah 41:10 "So do not fear, for I am with you; do not be dismayed, for I am your God. I will strengthen you and help you; I will uphold you with my righteous right hand" (NIV).*

Despite the difficult times and people, we must trust the process that God has put in His word, and we'll run and finish this race victoriously!

Prayer: *Heavenly Father, I thank you for your presence in my life. I thank you for your protection from the fiery darts that sometimes come in the form of "those" people. If I'm one of "those" people, please reveal it to me and help me pursue peace. I ask you to wrap your arms around everyone who feels hurt and alone. In your precious son's name, Jesus Christ! Amen!*

The Timing of Transformation

"Delight yourself also in the Lord, And He shall give you the desires of your heart. Commit your way to the Lord, Trust also in Him, And He shall bring it to pass" (Psalm 37: 4-5 NKJV).

While exploring with my grandson one day, we discovered a beautiful butterfly making its rounds through a patch of wildflowers. As I tried explaining to him how the butterfly came to be, I was reminded of the butterfly's transformation. Immediately I thought of the pain I often experience through life's challenges. I recognized the butterfly, and I had lots in common. We had come from a dark place to be—transformed.

The butterfly goes through several stages before becoming its final version. It seems like this insect symbolically goes through the same process we do by experiencing trials and tribulations.

The first stage of development of the butterfly is the larva stage, commonly known as caterpillars; no matter how long it takes, the caterpillar will continue to eat in preparation for the transition to the next step in its life cycle. No matter how long it takes for us to go through our lows, we should continue to stand on the word of God, adhering to the following scripture: *Be anxious for nothing, but in everything by prayer and supplication, with thanksgiving, let your requests be made known unto God* (Philippians 4: 6 NKJV).

The second stage is the pupa. During this stage, the caterpillar will break down entirely on a cellular level and then reorganize into a new form. Comparatively, God must allow us to go through our breakdowns to build our trust in him. As the word says, *And we know that all things work together for good to those who love God, to those who are the called according to His purpose (Romans 8:28 NKJV)*. We must therefore trust and believe that in everything we go through, God is working it out for our good.

Cont...The Timing of Transformation

The final stage is when the butterfly leaves behind their cocoon and takes to the air with its new wings. When this happens, we never see the butterfly crying about changing. Neither does it return to the darkness of the cocoon because those stages served their purpose. Likewise, when God brings us through times of night, we must surrender our past, desires, and worries to Him and then take flight.

Through it all, God hears our prayers and knows the desires of our hearts. He also knows what's best for us, including the timing for transformation. Nothing is better than trusting and believing in God's promises despite feeling like we're in the dark and broken down—because we're constantly being made new.

Prayer: *Heavenly Father, I thank you for your presence in my life. I thank you for keeping me through my darkest hours. Thank you for letting me see that you have given me peace to go through the valley of the shadow of death. I ask that you continue transforming me into the person you have called me to be. In Jesus' name, I pray. Amen!*

Keep Your Vision

Where there is no vision, the people perish: but he that keepeth the law, happy is he (Proverbs 29:18 KJV).

Where there is no revelation, people cast off restraint; but blessed is the one who heeds wisdom's instruction (Proverbs 29:18 NIV).

When you look at the word's meaning, vision has two implications. The first is "the faculty or state of being able to see." The second meaning, and the one my focus is on, says, "the ability to think about or plan the future with imagination or wisdom." Having an imagination is ok; it's what makes children happy when they use it. However, when you think about and plan your vision with "wisdom," you know that God is in the mix, and you cannot go wrong with Him.

You can be generally good, not bother anyone, and have people's best interests at heart. But there will still be individuals who don't see or understand your vision. If God gave you that vision and the wisdom to follow through, keep going until it comes to fruition.

I'm reminded of some of the lyrics to the song "He's Able" by Deitrick Vaughn Haddon: *God is able to do just what he said he would do. He's gonna fulfill every promise to you. Don't give up on God cause he won't give up on you. He's able.* Then it says, *Has anybody ever wanted to give up? Has anybody ever wanted to throw in the towel?* (Haddon). I've been there and done that, and God constantly flashes a vision he wants for my life in front of me.

I remember having a vision of wanting to give encouraging words and help people feel good about themselves. When God called me into the ministry, I kept saying for a long time — "I can't preach, write, or pray." I felt like no one would want to listen to me. Looking back, I can see I've always been hard on myself. Thankfully, God showed me that my ministry doesn't have to be behind a pulpit and that my gifts will make room for my vision. It's been a wonderful, spiritual feeling to receive messages from people regarding how a letter, communication with me, or our prayers together were life-changing.

Cont...Keep Your Vision

Sometimes we must encourage ourselves with God's word to stay focused on the goals of our vision. This scripture in either of these versions will give us the strength to keep going. 2nd Chronicles 15:7 (KJV) *Be ye strong therefore and let not your hands be weak: for your work shall be rewarded.* 2nd Chronicles 15:7 (NIV) *But as for you, be strong and do not give up, for your work will be rewarded."*

Let's trust God and work our vision, in Numbers 23:19 (KJV) says, *God is not a man, that he should lie; Neither the son of man, that he should repent: Hath he said, and shall he not do it? Or hath he spoken, and shall he not make it good?*

No matter what, let's work to keep our vision!

Prayer: Heavenly Father, I thank you for placing love for people in their lives in my heart. Please help me stay true to my vision and be a light to everyone I encounter. Help me to grow in your love and wisdom and to hold fast to your promises. In Jesus' name, AMEN!

A Healthy MIND, BODY, and SOUL

For as the body without the spirit is dead, so faith without works is dead also (James 2:26 KJV).

I'm a smart, beautiful, vivacious woman. I happen to be plus-sized, and I suffer with two serious health conditions. For most of my adult life, I'd believed being healthy meant being skinny. And being skinny meant being pretty. I'm not sure how the connection was made in my mind, but it has tormented me for years.

Things had gotten to the point where I'd become so defensive, I assumed any discussion about my weight and health was really a personal attack. All I could hear were words, I'd begun to think about myself: *you're ugly*. Also, I have Polycystic ovary syndrome (PCOS). This condition makes losing weight a lot harder. In fact, PCOS makes you gain weight. However, losing weight will help with PCOS.

In recent times, I decided to attend counseling. My favorite scripture justifying this level of self-care is James 2: 26, because the word instructs me to exercise my faith. When I feel defensive or weak I say to myself, "God is here for me, but he also created people I can depend on in times of need." I often forget that I need to apply that same thinking to my physical and spiritual health as well. Learning to love the skin I'm in has been a long process–with the help of the Lord, I'm getting through it. As I've been on this journey, I've learned to embrace the parts of me I've typically rejected. I'm working to be increasingly accountable and take ownership for my habits and choices, as these past few months have been a real eye opener for me.

Cont...A Healthy MIND, BODY, and SOUL

In February 2021, I was hospitalized and diagnosed with extra fluid in my head. The two biggest causes of this condition are: (1) being a female of child-bearing age (2) being overweight. This diagnosis made me realize I needed to gain better control over my health. This month I have been taking steps in that direction. I still eat too many sweets on occasion. However, I am working out 3 times a week. I try to drink ½ gallon of water a day (I fail some days, but I am drinking more than I used to). I also pick out healthier lunches. This process is a journey, but I know that putting in the work and seeking Jesus, is the only way to get a healthy mind, body, and soul.

I cannot just pray myself thin (I've tried)...faith without works is dead!

Prayer: Heavenly Father, I thank you for helping me through this process of loving myself the way you love me. Help me to continue to strive for a healthy mind, body, and soul. In Jesus' name I pray, Amen!

Christlike in Social Media

So be careful how you live. Don't live like fools, but like those who are wise. Make the most of every opportunity in these evil days (Eph. 5:15-16 NLT).

From a very young age, I've loved technology. Being a shy person, I like using a screen to help me communicate with others. Some have said that we spend too much time behind a screen, but all I see is how much more open the world is for me. Before the pandemic hit, I searched for a church home in this new city I'm in with my mom and sister. The pandemic hit and brought that search to a halt. Technology gave us the ability to connect with our church home several states away.

There is a positive and negative outcome in our world of technology and social media. Let me take a little of your time and break down Ephesians 5:15-16 in the way that the holy spirit revealed it to me.

"So be careful how you live:" This means how we live off and on social media, pay attention to what we put on your social media pages. Is it uplifting to others? Is it edifying Christ?

"Don't live like fools, but like those who are wise:" This scripture tells us to be mindful of every aspect of our lives. Just because what we're saying is the truth doesn't give us the right to be mean-spirited and messy. We should continually examine the way we use our words. Even when sharing images, just because we think a picture is okay doesn't mean it's appropriate as we may be sharing the wrong message.

"Make the most of every opportunity in these evil days:" These days, especially with the pandemic and people staying away from each other socially, technology has become the way to keep connected. Because of my medical condition and low immune system, I am completing my bachelor's online, attending church online, and communicating with my friends online. It may not be ideal, but I am making the most of every opportunity these days, like many of us.

Cont...Christlike in Social Media

Here's the bottom line: in all that I do, I should watch what I put on social media because:

⇒ Employers check out their employee's social media sites

⇒ What people see about me on social media shapes their perspective of who I am

⇒ Who I am should reflect Christ

⇒ My image matters

⇒ God sees it all. I can't hide from him

Dear Lord, help me to continue to trust in the guidance that you give me. Help me always think of you on social media to demonstrate your love for the world consistently. I ask that you bless this world with love and peace as we go through difficult times. In Jesus' name, I pray, AMEN.

Let Him Guide You!

You'll travel safely, you'll neither tire nor trip. 24 You'll take afternoon naps without a worry, you'll enjoy a good night's sleep. 25 No need to panic over alarms or surprises, or predictions that doomsday's just around the corner. 26 Because God will be right there with you; he'll keep you safe and sound **(Proverbs 3:23-26 The Message).**

The trip I took this past week was in honor of my dad who passed away three years ago. He had planned to take a vacation with my mom. Their original plan was to stop at different locations and enjoy life and each other. They were not able to do it, so my sister, my mom, and I did it. During this trip, I learned a lot about allowing Jesus to guide me. However, there are two things I discovered that stood out to me. They are:

He will take you where you need to go and not always were you want to go.

I did not want to have a vacation in Muncie, Indiana because I honestly didn't think we would have a nice time. Although we'd planned to drop off my cousins and leave immediately, God had other plans. We were able to visit many people who appeared genuinely happy to see us.

He showed me that we should stop when and where we are needed.

We were going to get our hotel room and then call a lady the same evening. She was someone we hadn't seen since moving from Louisiana. Our plan had been to visit with her the following day. God had other plans. We called her while sitting outside her house. She had tears in her eyes when she opened the door, a sure sign, she was pleased to see us. That made me feel good.

Cont...Let Him Guide You!

In my travels through life, I've ventured down good roads, had detours, and also taken some rough roads. The move to Florida has been challenging, but I keep hearing the conversation that my dad had with my mom; "God doesn't always put us in a place to learn the good of it, sometimes he wants us to learn from the bad." "What"...learn from the bad? But I learned that when things are going bad, I need to put my Hope and Trust in the Lord.

When I feel like I am not welcomed in a place and my anxiety gets high, I am reminded of His word in *Psalm 32:7-8 (NLT), 7 For you are my hiding place; you protect me from trouble. You surround me with songs of victory. 8 The Lord says, "I will guide you along the best pathway for your life. I will advise you and watch over you.* I know that God is with me, I am looking at what he would like me to learn, and I have the assurance that he will guide me through this stage of my life.

Prayer: *Father God, I thank you for the hope I have in you. I thank you for being my hiding place and for protecting my mind and soul! Continue to guide me on the path that you have for me. Do not let me become weary and swallowed up by the disappointments of my life. Amen!*

He Has The Blueprint!

"For I know the plans I have for you," declares the Lord, "plans to prosper you and not to harm you, plans to give you hope and a future" (Jeremiah 29:11 NIV).

Jeremiah 29:11 is one of the many beautiful promises made by God to us. It is a promise that although we'll experience suffering and hardship, there's a long-term plan of hope and prosperity. We are God's "blueprint." He knows everything we have to go through to build us the way He needs us to be made. We must have the patience to go through the building of our faith.

A few months ago, I was rushed to the hospital by ambulance for suspected food poisoning. Upon arrival, I had to wait in the hallway for a room in the ER. Then I had to stay in the ER room until a room was available on the observation wing. I was in pain, my blood pressure was elevated, and my migraine was so bad. I wasn't allowed to have any medication until my primary doctor came to the hospital the next day. When I was moved to a regular room, I wasn't allowed to have anything to eat or drink for three days. My doctor decided to continue to withhold medication. Instead, I was given IV antibiotics to fight a dangerous infection.

At the time, I believed the staff could've made me feel better by providing my medication. I didn't consider that the discomfort I was going through temporarily was meant for my good. They needed to treat the infection to save my life before giving me the medication that would've made me comfortable.

My experience made me think of situations in the bible where people endured discomfort for a time while God worked in the background to preserve them for the future. Though the Israelites were slaves to the Egyptians, God told them to build houses, plant gardens, and marry. In other words, God was telling them that although their situation was uncomfortable, to be content in the place they were, and they'd be delivered to a land of promise. Eventually, God brought the Israelites out of Egypt into the promised land.

Cont...He Has The Blueprint!

I initially thought I was being taken to the hospital for food poisoning. I felt awful when my blood pressure elevated, and I struggled with a migraine. However, those issues were secondary compared to the deadly infection ravaging my body. Therefore, the suffering that I had to go through first was needed to get my body healed. The doctors created a plan or a blueprint for my care.

In the same way, God does the same for us as he has the blueprint for our lives and knows best. He'll never take us places or through illnesses without equipping us to manage our challenges. We know this to be true because of his words in Ephesians 2:10 (NIV) *"For we are God's handiwork, created in Christ Jesus to do good works, which God prepared in advance for us to do."*

Prayer: *Heavenly Father, thank you for the many promises you've given me. Please help me continue to be about your business despite the discomforts of life. Please help me find peace through my challenges, knowing that you have the blueprint for my life and know best. Please show me how to encourage others and accept encouragement when needed. In your son Jesus' name, I pray. Amen!*

Wisdom-God's Guarantee!

"Plans fail for lack of counsel, but with many advisers they succeed" (Pro. 15:22 NIV).

"Trust in the Lord with all your heart and lean not on your own understanding; in all your ways submit to him, and he will make your paths straight" (Pro. 3:5-6 NIV).

One thing I struggle with is asking for help. I always assume that it is a sign of weakness because I am at an age where I should have my stuff together. I've been working on this issue within myself for years. Proverbs 15:22 says, *plans fail for lack of counsel, but with many advisers they succeed.* I know from experience that this is the case.

During college, I struggled with specific homework assignments because I thought I was supposed to do it all independently. It got to a point where any project that involved writing would cripple me with anxiety to the end of failing a couple of classes.

While teaching, I refused to reach out to the administration when I was struggling for fear of seeming incapable of doing my job. This brought about extreme anxiety that I was not a good and effective teacher.

Recently I had a conversation with my mother about a car I was interested in purchasing. She was surprised because I had never mentioned it before. The irony is I have wanted that particular vehicle for ten years. I realized that I was not seeing my dreams come to fruition by not speaking up about the simple things. It struck me that I'd repeated this same mistake with God.

I've shut people out of my life who genuinely love and support me, people who could've provided wise counsel when I needed it most. And if I've done that with friends and family, how much more do I falter when I do that with Him? How can I expect God to give me the desires of my heart, if I shut Him out?

Cont...Wisdom-God's Guarantee!

So, I'm spending my time now learning to reach out to others when I am struggling and to pray and seek God as well. And to trust the process!

***Prayer:** Father God, I come to you with so much thanksgiving in my heart for showing me that I don't have to be perfect. I can lean on you, and you will direct me to whom I need to reach out to for your godly counsel. Bless all that needs to be on the right path to trust your process. In Jesus' name, Amen!*

It's Okay To Mourn

***Psalm 59:16 NIV** But I will sing of your strength, in the morning I will sing of your love; for you are my fortress, my refuge in times of trouble.*

For many years I've been a minister. I've naturally been a person always in the position of helping others going through difficult times. But, one day I went to a dark place. I did not know how to express myself after I lost my husband. I went through so many different emotions. At times it seemed like the pain was—unbearable.

I got to the point when I asked, "God, I don't understand why this was happening to me?" As Christians, I believe we can all struggle with thinking it shows weakness in our faith if we cry or mourn too long. I was reminded of, Matthew 5:4 *Blessed are those who mourn, for they will be comforted.* Yes, it is "OKAY TO MOURN."

While I was going through this tragedy, "Hallelujah" I had the word down on the inside of me. Even though I was unable to read my bible, I was able to call up the word of God and draw strength on His word. You see, even as Christian we will have trials and tribulations. We are not immune from hurt and pain. But if we can hold onto the promises of God—He will see us through all the difficult times in our lives.

***Prayer:** Heavenly Father, I come to You giving all praise and honor for Your love and protection over our lives. Father God, I ask that You put Your loving arms around those needing strength and comfort in these times of despair. Let Your word be a light unto our path. In Jesus, Your precious son's name, I pray. Thank You, God, and Amen!*

Better Than The Beginning

"If you are depressed, you are living in the past. If you are anxious, you are living in the future. If you are at peace, you are living in the present" — Lao Tzu.

I often struggle with bouts of depression and anxiety. Honestly, it's no fun. I feel like I'm in a dark underground tunnel with no way to escape. Climbing out of a depressive state isn't easy, and healing anxious thoughts sometimes seems even more complex. However, I talk about what I've been through with both because I hope that I can help others deal with their issues by sharing my story.

The end of a matter is better than its beginning, and patience is better than pride (Ecclesiastes 7:8 NIV).

After rereading this scripture, I had a breakthrough moment—realizing my lack of patience had been significantly contributing to depression and anxiety. I knew I had to do things differently for the peace I wanted to flood my heart and change my life.

Growing up, I always had big dreams for my life and where I would be by certain ages. I wanted to have my first child before I turned 27 because my mother had waited to start her family, and it was a matter that her family always brought up. I wanted to have kids close in age with my sisters so that my kids would be close in age with their cousins and could be friends. I wanted to be set in my career by 25 because that's what many mainstream shows and movies depicted as what a competent adult looked like.

When my dad passed, I was broken. The biggest goal I wanted to achieve was having kids before either one of my parents died. Seeing each of those missed milestones as I got older wounded me. I was upset at my past self for not working harder to reach those goals. I was worried about whether I would ever get to the future that I saw for myself.

Cont...Better Than The Beginning

My father died young. As devastating as this was for my siblings and me, it was a horrible blow to my mother. I believe his death dredged up the remembrance of her mother's untimely death. I saw how much losing a parent affected my mother. Hearing stories of my grandmother, for whom I am named, has been a bittersweet challenge. Her early death meant I missed the opportunity to have a relationship with her. This was also a hard thing to deal with growing up.

My recent prayers have motivated me to ask God for strength to forgive myself for my past and to have more patience to wait for the ending he has in store. I trust that the rest of my life always has the potential to be better than the beginning!

The words of Ecclesiastes 7:8 is a constant reminder to us that despite the hardships, we have God's promises to look forward to. While doing so, we're building our faith by exercising patience. Though I've combated deep regret, sadness, and remorse, there's hope on the horizon. Likewise, many of us may be struggling now, but it is only the start of God's plans for us. No matter our age or position in life, God has a bright future planned. One that's so much better than anything we could have dreamed of.

Prayer: *Father God, I thank you for being an on-time God. It may not be my timing, but your timing is always right. I thank you for forgiving me and teaching me how to forgive myself. I ask that you continue to lead me down this path you have just for me and allow me to be a light for others. In your son Jesus' name, I pray. Amen!*

www.ingramcontent.com/pod-product-compliance
Lightning Source LLC
LaVergne TN
LVHW010415070526
838199LV00064B/5303